What Our Readers Have Said...

Applicability

"These books are great tools that should be used as guidelines for our everyday supervisory practices. You need to take the time to do a short self-evaluation when reading them."

•

"The Pinpoint Training Series delivers information that could be used in a lot different areas."

•

"The things and problems we deal with everyday are discussed in these books."

Convenience

"I like this because I can take them with me to read at a convenient time. I feel the little time I have to spend in the office is best use on activities that directly relate to revenue opportunities. I like the short amount of time it takes to keep up with these."

•

"I prefer the self-study approach; it fits in with my schedule."

•

"I like the fact that the format allows the books to be reviewed as time permits. All work has been conducted on personal, evening/weekend time."

•

"Easy to use... if you put the time into it."

Challenge

"My thought is that the real value of these books comes into effect when doing the action plans."

•

"I like the fact that the format allows assignments to be reviewed as time permits."

Clarity

"Short and sweet. These books are easy to comprehend."

•

"Easy to use, understand, and reference if needed."

Relevance

"I have enjoyed reading these books. They are relevant to today's work environment and the ongoing change in the way we manage our workforce."

•

"I believe the contents of the Pinpoint series are excellent. It causes one to reflect on the daily dynamics in working with oneself as well as with management and peers."

Building & Nurturing Trust in the Workplace

Pinpoint Leadership Skill Development Training Series

TIMOTHY F. BEDNARZ

MAJORIUM
BUSINESS PRESS

Pinpoint Leadership Skill Development Training Series
"Building & Nurturing Trust in the Workplace"
Timothy F. Bednarz

Graphic design: Monika Pawlak

Majorium Business Press
2025 Main Street
Stevens Point, WI 54481
715.342.1018 • 800.654.4935

ISBN 978-1-882181-51-3

Printed in the United States of America

Introduction

The Pinpoint Leadership Skill Development Training Series is designed for targeted training and education regarding increased improvement in a specific skill or competency.

Each book within this series is designed to be easy to use, understand and apply to your job. It can be used as a basis for training individuals, as a discussion guide or as a personal training tool.

Each chapter within this book discusses a specific concept. When you have completed all eight chapters you should have a 360° perspective of the topic.

Additionally, each chapter is divided into specific sections:

- The first section provides you with an overview of the topic
- The Implications section discusses why the concept is important, and why it is important to learn and apply.
- The Strategies, Tips & Techniques to Apply section teaches how to use and apply the particular concept to your work.
- The Points to Ponder section gives you something to think about or to be discussed with a group setting. These are questions not meant to be immediately answered, but to be pondered over time.
- The Training Activity section provides you with the tools to transfer what you have learned to your job. It is designed to help create an action plan to effectively apply the concept.

Each of the topics in this series is time-tested and proven in the marketplace. They have been used by thousands of employees as training tools. Many of the users have commented that what made these books valuable, was the ability to refer to them when a problem surfaced. They indicated that they remembered reading about the exact problem. They referred back to these books and found an appropriate solution.

You will find them equally valuable as a resource in your professional development library.

Table of Contents

LEARNING OBJECTIVES:

- To identify and apply the elements, factors and principles defining trust.
- To interpret and analyze the critical factors and benefits of trust.
- To identify the implications and ramifications of trust and its impact upon the leader and their organization.
- To overcome problems and pitfalls related to issues of trust.
- To apply specific strategies to enhance the development of trust in a leader and within the workplace.

1

Defining the Role of Trust in Leadership

As seen in numerous large-scale corporate scandals around the turn of the century, trust or a lack thereof has a dramatic impact on the organization. While an organization can be defined as trusting and empowering, it is the individuals within it who form the basis for these qualities.

The responsibility for fostering and nurturing trust does not lie with the bottom tiers of the organization, but the leaders that lead it. Where there is no trust, there is no legitimacy to leadership.

The starting point is the personal commitment made by individual leaders.

IMPLICATIONS — WHAT THIS MEANS TO YOU

Trust and empowerment stem from the individual actions of a leader. However, once initiated, trust and empowerment create a synergy within the organization that has the ability to move it forward to unimaginable heights.

As soon as employees know they can trust the words and actions of their leaders, they are motivated. All too often the words sound good, but the accompanying actions do not follow, fostering a sense of mistrust and fear within employees.

Once leaders have established trust with their employees, a strong bond is formed that is difficult to break. Unless trust is broken and people feel betrayed, employees will be intensely loyal and cooperate to achieve mutual goals and objectives. This is the strongest principle of leadership and its essence.

STRATEGIES, TIPS & TECHNIQUES TO APPLY

Whether or not a leader is trusted is determined by his or her actions. Anyone can make statements and pronouncements; it is the actions by which an individual is judged. Leaders must hold to higher standards of personal behavior if they are to foster and nurture trust with their employees, who closely observe every word and action.

Leaders are judged by the following criteria:

Promises and Commitments

Leaders in the corporate world are placed under an enormous amount of stress and will miss commitments, especially minor ones made in the heat of daily activities. However, leaders pay close attention to what they say, and they do what they promise. If unable to keep their commitment, they immediately inform the other party and make alternative arrangements.

Employees take note of a leader who makes a personal commitment but fails to keep it due to political or internal pressures. If when confronted with this failure they make excuses rather than take responsibility, they will be perceived as hypocritical. Employees with little other alternative may accept the excuse, but will inwardly feel betrayed and no longer trust the leader. The foundation for leadership has been greatly undermined.

Mistakes

As part of the human condition, everybody makes mistakes and fails. When leaders make mistakes, they often impact and affect their organization. Trust is established when leaders openly acknowledge their mistakes to their employees and apologize for them.

Leaders also allow their employees to experiment, make mistakes and fail without repercussions. They foster an atmosphere where employees can learn from their mistakes and move on. Leaders understand that individuals can only grow when they are allowed to learn. The most effective learning experiences stem not from successes but failures and mistakes.

Loyalty

Leaders give and demand loyalty from their employees. While they understand that loyalty is earned, they do not tolerate employees who are disloyal to their organization and each other.

The most open demonstration of a leader's own lack of loyalty can be seen in his or her constant and open criticism of superiors and employees in their absence. While loyalty is not blind, leaders must demonstrate, at all times, a deep sense of allegiance to the organization, superiors, associates and employees.

If a leader takes issue with the actions of others, they should openly but privately discuss it with the individual and not criticize them behind his or her back.

Information

Leaders show faith in their employees when they share information with them. In many organizations, the control of information is the basis of personal power. Leaders understand that employees must be informed if they are to do their job well and be empowered to make decisions affecting their work. Leaders who withhold information, clearly demonstrate their mistrust of their employees.

Involvement

Trust is established with employees when they are included and empowered to make decisions that affect them. Trust is undermined when employees are enabled to make decisions but the decisions are never acted upon and implemented.

Effective leaders actively work with their employees and trust their decisions. They work with their employees in implementing them and striving toward the accomplishment of mutual goals and objectives.

Recognition

Trust is fostered and nurtured when leaders recognize the individual contributions of their employees and publicly recognize them for their efforts.

When new ideas and strategies work, leaders never accept credit for the idea. They always acknowledge the efforts and contributions of their employees. To do otherwise betrays the trust of those employees.

Communication

Leaders build trust within their organization by maintaining open communication with all employees, superiors and associates. They understand that trust is only established when they communicate regardless of the situation and circumstances, and whether or not the information is positive or negative.

Goals and objectives are effectively met when all involved have a complete picture of what is happening around them, including the barriers and obstacles to be overcome.

Respect Confidentiality

Leaders understand trust is developed when they respect and honor confidential and sensitive information provided to them by superiors, associates and employees.

They also know they must trust their employees with the confidential and sensitive information they need to do their jobs and make quality decisions. Without this confidence, leaders will not be able to create a trusting environment since they are evincing a basic suspicion of their employees.

POINTS TO PONDER — SOMETHING TO THINK ABOUT

1. How would you rate your personal level of trustworthiness?
2. How would you evaluate the atmosphere in your organization?

TRAINING ACTIVITY — APPLICATION & ACTION PLAN

1. Perform a self-analysis regarding trust. On a sheet of paper list the following:
    - Promises and commitments
    - Mistakes
    - Loyalty
    - Information
    - Involvement
    - Credit
    - Communications
    - Respect confidentiality
2. Next to each category, list ways you can increase your personal levels of trust and foster trust with your employees.
3. Identify the actions you need to take to implement your ideas.

2

The Impact of Trust on Organizations

The overall effects of trust reach deeply into any organization. Trust is the key element and core of leadership. It is the foundation upon which all other leadership competencies are based, and the basis for all human interaction at all levels from employees to customers. Both motivation and loyalty are based upon trust. Leaders and their organizations cannot function without it.

IMPLICATIONS — WHAT THIS MEANS TO YOU

Trust is at the heart of leadership. The faith placed in a leader by superiors, associates and employees stems directly from his or her personal trustworthiness. With the development of mutual trust, employees are motivated to take additional steps to support each other in the accomplishment of shared goals and objectives.

The factors that establish and sustain trust can never be compromised. It is what defines a leader's character and competence. As a keystone of leadership, anything that diminishes mutual trust works to undermine and eventually destroy the ability to lead.

STRATEGIES, TIPS & TECHNIQUES TO APPLY

A sound organization is built upon a trusting environment. This builds strong relationships of faith in one another, empowerment, performance and a shared vision resulting in the following benefits:

Increased Personal Trust

Leaders who develop a high-trust environment are working on multiple levels to create trust in themselves, superiors, associates, employees, suppliers and customers. They understand the establishment of trust begins with themselves, then flows to all levels of their organization. Trust is not an organizational function but a personal one. Once established it can then be cultivated one individual at a time. It means keeping promises and honoring commitments, acknowledging mistakes, demonstrating loyalty, openly communicating with others and maintaining confidences.

Leadership demands that leaders stand up for their personal values and beliefs despite potential negative consequences. When others see a leader's unwavering commitment, personal levels of trust and confidence increase. People know they are able to trust and believe a leader's words and actions. This is an immeasurable, priceless quality that can enable an organization to rise to great heights.

Strengthened Relationships

An environment of trust strengthens all personal relationships in the business. This occurs because as increasing levels of trust are reached, promises and commitments are kept, faith in and loyalty to each other is established, communication improved and mistakes openly acknowledged.

A synergy is established as individuals in the organization are bonded together by deeper levels of trust. Each develops an understanding that he or she can count on others to do their job and can deal with them openly, honestly and with integrity. This establishes an organizational cohesiveness that is indispensable to attaining mutual goals and objectives.

Improved Communication

Higher levels of trust beget better communication within the organization. In high-trust environments information is shared with the people who need it at all levels because it is common knowledge they can be trusted to apply the information appropriately. Communication channels are also opened to include all levels of employees, regardless of their position or authority.

Improved communication in an environment of mutual trust allows both leaders and employees to openly admit and acknowledge personal mistakes, learn from them and move on free of repercussion. It also acknowledges that employees at all levels can be trusted to honor confidential and sensitive information. This empowers employees and actively involves them in the decisions affecting them.

Sustained Positive Change

As trust and open communication are firmly rooted in the organizational culture, leaders are able to effect ongoing positive change. This occurs as organizational cohesiveness is established and all employees are motivated by a shared vision of what the organization can realize through the attainment of mutual goals and objectives. All employees trust their leaders and organization to recognize their accomplishments and contributions and do not fear someone else being given credit for their work.

Decreased Frustrations

As a spirit of trust and open communication is achieved, leaders will experience a decrease in frustrations and resistance as dysfunctional relationships are eliminated and group trust is established. Since employees at all levels are empowered and included in decision making, many problems are diminished and eliminated.

Increased Commitment

Increased levels of trust and organizational cohesiveness foster higher levels of commitment within the organization. As individual employees learn to work and trust each other as a unit, and see the positive results from their combined efforts, many will begin to contribute new ideas and feedback on how to better the organization. A synergy of trust, commitment and communication nurtures and sustains this positive momentum.

Reduction of Internal Politics

Internal politics, infighting and turf wars occur because individuals do not trust the organization to recognize and reward their contributions. Consequently, they begin to take control of their circumstances and use deceptive tactics to obtain what they feel is legitimately theirs.

An environment of trust eliminates or drastically reduces the negative impact of personal and internal politics. The atmosphere of trust bonds all leaders and employees together and isolates parties who wish to be enmeshed in office politics. These individuals quickly learn that the rules have changed and that they must learn to cooperate rather than agitate—or leave the organization. The environment no longer tolerates time and energy-wasting internal politics since the focus has naturally shifted from the individual to the organization.

This does not imply individuals are consumed by and lost to the organization, only that as the provider of livelihoods its good is put first, and maneuvering, the rumor mill, backbiting and other game playing are seen as useless pitfalls to avoid at all costs.

Improved Quality

The building of trust is the key to high-performing organizations. Strong and sustainable levels of trust transform the organization, increasing its effectiveness, productivity and the overall quality of the product or service being produced. This occurs because personal animosity and problems are eliminated or at least fade well into the background. Employees are motivated to increase the quality of their products and services because trust has empowered them to be a vital part of the organization. They are treated with respect and trusted to be a contributing part of the organization. This increases their personal satisfaction and loyalty to the organization.

POINTS TO PONDER — SOMETHING TO THINK ABOUT

1. What is the level of trust within the organizational unit that you lead?
2. Do you personally trust your superiors, associates and employees? Explain.

TRAINING ACTIVITY — APPLICATION & ACTION PLAN

1. Examine the key benefits of trust listed in this lesson and identify how increased trust can be beneficial to your organization within each area.
2. Determine how you can begin to increase individual levels of trust. Identify the actions you can personally take to establish an encompassing atmosphere of trust.

3

The Implications of Trust in the Workplace

The need for trust in the workplace and communication therein is understood by many leaders to be the foundational building block of the organization. The degree of trust developed will impact employee performance and retention, the development of teams and implementation of organizational change. Irrespective of size and industry, organizations are comprised of individuals who desire the same thing: the ability to trust those they work with. People cannot trust an organization, but they can trust their superiors, employees and associates.

IMPLICATIONS — WHAT THIS MEANS TO YOU

Issues of broken trust and personal betrayal are far from just the result of restructuring, downsizing or other major organizational events. They are the product of the numerous micro-decisions that leaders and managers make every day. When individuals do not keep agreements or remain true to their word, and do not share information or trust another employee's judgment or competence, trust is breached. Employees develop feelings of betrayal that lead to a chain of unresolved conflicts. These unresolved conflicts build a strong sense of mistrust and disloyalty that is extremely difficult to counteract.

This is important for leaders because they are personally responsible for developing the trust needed to bind their organization together into a cohesive unit. They have the personal ability to control the series of micro-decisions that contribute to a sense of mistrust and undermine their ability to lead. With their personal words and actions, they have the power to build or destroy their employee's faith. They are the ones who must know that every statement or decision, no matter how inconsequential it may appear at the time, has an effect on whether or not corporate goals are reached.

STRATEGIES, TIPS & TECHNIQUES TO APPLY

Feelings of broken trust and betrayal are not just the byproducts of cataclysmic organizational change. They happen every day, and are in fact so pervasive that studies conducted since the mid-1940s have consistently shown that employees seem to have higher needs for esteem, respect and self-actualization, while most employers feel concerned only for their employees' salary and safety. This demonstrates a clear disconnect that has implications for the future of organizations.

There is an increased need for trust in organizations as the world and corporate environments continue to change. Both organizational structures and managerial practices are changing and these changes do not appear to be ending in the near term. The policies and traditions that cemented employees to a company, which they relied upon, have disappeared. They have all exacted a high price in the form of diminishing employee loyalty and trust.

Many managers and leaders will quickly attribute the lack of loyalty to employee job-hopping. Yet the 2001 *Randstad North American Employee Review* reported that 77% of employees polled defined success as "a long-term commitment with one company."

The lack of trust in many work environments is pervasive. Restructuring, mergers and acquisitions have produced not only opportunity, but also uncertainty and anxiety. Individuals in the current climate feel that they are unable to trust their future, their organization or even themselves.

Leaders need to create open and flexible organizations that are able to readily adapt to rapidly changing conditions. All indications point to organizational environments becoming more complex as changes and global pressures become more intense. While this places tremendous stress on the organization, leaders must also respond to their employees' needs in a way that honors relationships and builds trust.

Change requires organizations to become agile and flexible. This demands employees who are willing to take risks. Taking risks requires employees that are able to trust themselves, their capabilities, and decisions as well as their leaders, coworkers and organizations.

Leaders must learn to evaluate their employees to determine their capacity for trust. This means establishing a foundation for trust that demands that past unsettled conflicts be resolved before a solid foundation for trust can be built. It also means that leaders must be conscious of their daily practices that either make or break employee trust.

The dynamics of trust are complex. It takes time and effort to develop trust and one small event to lose it. Regaining lost trust, while extremely difficult, is a critical element in any relationship. By first trusting themselves and others, it is possible for leaders to then develop caring, genuine relationships and rebuild trust with their employees.

When trust is ignored, the pain and price is tremendous, as it is the key to all successful change initiatives within the organization. Without trust, change will be difficult if not impossible to achieve.

POINTS TO PONDER — SOMETHING TO THINK ABOUT

1. How critical do you perceive the element of trust to be within your organization?
2. Do you pay attention to the concept of trust or do you take it for granted?

TRAINING ACTIVITY — APPLICATION & ACTION PLAN

Consider the role of trust within your organization by examining your daily management practices.

1. Identify what are you doing to build trust with your employees.
2. Identify the actions that may be betraying your employee's trust.
3. Identify the actions and activities you can personally take to resolve past problems and build new levels of trust with your employees.

4

Common Pitfalls Associated with Trust-Building in the Workplace

Leaders can be so caught up in the flurry of daily tasks and activities that they easily stumble into many pitfalls resulting in broken trusts with and betrayals of employees. Many of these actions are inadvertent, yet consequences can compound over time as unresolved conflicts build in employees' minds.

The desire for building trust is an attitude that leaders either have or must develop if they wish to be successful. It is an essential building block of leadership. If leaders are unable to nurture a workplace grounded in an appreciation for the power of trust, instead of lead they will only be able to manage and direct using fear as the primary motivator.

IMPLICATIONS — WHAT THIS MEANS TO YOU

This is important for leaders to appreciate because of the ease in which they can stumble into past management practices that undermine rather than cultivate employee trust. It may take time and effort to foster a personal attitude of trust, but when leaders do they will find their employees more effective, cooperative and productive. The alternative is an atmosphere of mistrust and betrayal where continual conflict, ineffectiveness and quality problems reign—and worsen over time.

STRATEGIES, TIPS & TECHNIQUES TO APPLY

Many leaders can easily stumble into a myriad of pitfalls and practices that undermine their ability to build and foster trust with their employees. The stress and demands of daily work make it easy for a leader to overlook many of their actions without understanding their attendant consequences. These can include:

Inconsistency

When leaders are reactive rather than proactive, they are often inconsistent in their actions. A decision made in reaction to a specific event or circumstance can be inconsistent with a similar decision made at another time. While both may seem logical at the time, this inconsistency creates a sense of mistrust in employees since they have little or no idea what to expect from the leader's behavior.

Other inconsistencies occur when leaders show favoritism toward one employee over another. Employees don't feel they are treated fairly and, consequently, will not trust the leader's judgment.

Reluctance to Share Information

Many managers and leaders are reluctant to share facts and figures with their employees because they feel unable to trust them with the information. This attitude clearly and completely sets the tone in the organization. If a leader shares information freely, he or she will find that employees will in turn begin to share information with them. This builds an atmosphere of mutual trust and open communication.

The leader reluctant to trust employees with information shuts down this critical two-way communication and limits the organization's ability to grow and adapt to change.

Lack of Personal Trust

Leaders must learn to trust their own personal judgment and competency.

They must accept that they will make mistakes, be willing to learn from them, and move on.

As leaders face a daily barrage of information, feedback and data, they must learn to take time out of the day to do nothing but "let the dust settle." This enables them to see things more clearly and in their entirety, to identify what needs to be done, and as time spent with employees is usually more important than any other item on the agenda, where time needs to be spent in order to build trust.

Lack of Open Dialogue

Building or rebuilding trust among employees is one of the biggest challenges leaders face. Downsizing and mergers have taken a toll on workplace trust, making employees more territorial wondering if they need to work to protect their jobs. Leaders must acknowledge these fears and anxieties and open a dialogue allowing employees to vent their fears and anxieties.

Refusal to Deal with the Past

Many leaders feel that the past events and circumstances that may have caused employees to feel betrayed are just that—in the past, and should be ignored. Yet it is a clear mistake to ignore these unresolved conflicts, as they will continue to fester and undermine any efforts to reestablish trust.

As leaders open a dialogue with employees, these issues should be allowed to surface and be dealt with. While it is true that the past cannot be changed, these personal feelings must be resolved before trust can be truly established.

Lack of Clarity of Beliefs and Values

In the heat of organizational change, the beliefs and values of the organization can get lost or muddled. Leaders must take the time to clarify fundamental beliefs and translate them into commonly held and agreed upon values. This allows leaders to align their organization with the company's values and beliefs.

POINTS TO PONDER — SOMETHING TO THINK ABOUT

1. What trust-building pitfalls give you the most trouble? Why?
2. What is the most successful way for you to build trust with your employees?

TRAINING ACTIVITY — APPLICATION & ACTION PLAN

In order to create more trusting relationships, and subsequently, more satisfaction:

1. Write down five things you have done in the last month to build trust in your workplace.
2. Write down five things you will do to build trust in the next thirty days.

5

Leadership Is Build on Trust

The actions and behaviors of individual leaders impact trust within the organization. Many fail to understand the elements of a trusting work atmosphere and the strategies used to build and establish a firm foundation for trust and leadership.

There are five key elements a leader must focus their efforts on to develop a comprehensive atmosphere of trust in their workplace. While the concept of trust implies participation by both leader and the people they deal with, including their superiors, associates, peers and employees, it must start with the individual leader. It is counterproductive for leaders to withhold their trust until they are able to trust the other party. In most cases trust is mutually developed by both parties and balanced by the commitment each brings to the relationship. Typically, employees and other individuals will reciprocate the trust placed in them by leaders.

IMPLICATIONS — WHAT THIS MEANS TO YOU

As leaders attempt to build trust, they will experience reluctance in the form of employees who have felt betrayed by the organization in the past. Consequently, leaders must signal a change by making the first steps to initiate and demonstrate trust in their employees. Once employees see that a true change has occurred, they will begin to slowly form the bonds of trust needed for leaders to be effective.

STRATEGIES, TIPS & TECHNIQUES TO APPLY

Leaders who wish to establish a complete environment of trust with their superiors, associates, peers and employees must consider employing the following strategies:

Establish Professional and Personal Credibility

If leaders are credible, they are trusted and believable to their employees. Employees consider a credible leader to be one who does not advance a personal agenda but has the best interests of the organization and his or her employees at heart.

Employees and other individuals view credibility from differing perspectives. Often credibility can be confused with personal competence. If the leader is knowledgeable and possesses both personal expertise and experience, they are considered credible. Conversely, leaders who maintain positions in which they demonstrate professional incompetence exhibit a lack of professional credibility, with employees viewing their direction, judgment and leadership as suspect.

The other aspect is the leader's own personal credibility. This involves the employee's ability to personally trust what a leader says or does. An individual may possess professional credibility and not possess the personal credibility to lead the organization. Strategies leaders must apply to develop and foster personal credibility include:

- Making themselves available to their employees and easy to talk with. Good leaders do not wait for their employees to approach them, but seek them out on a regular basis. Many will walk around and talk with each employee several times a day to discuss everyday concerns and issues. This proactive approach allows them to monitor the pulse of their organization while facilitating open communication with their employees. They instantly answer questions with straight responses and openly make their expectations of the organization and their employees known.
- Trusting their employees to handle their jobs and responsibilities

without regularly looking over their shoulders and micro-managing their activities.

- Being completely reliable and always delivering on their promises and commitments without fail, enabling employees to know without question that they can count on the leader.

Fairness

Trust is built when employees know their leader is fair and consistent in his or her actions, decisions and judgments—no matter who is involved and what the circumstances.

Fairness is comprised of both equity and consistency. Leaders can use the following strategies to develop a strong sense of equity including:

- Ensuring all employees are treated in the same manner.
- Making sure all actions, judgments and decisions are fair to all parties concerned.
- Avoiding any favoritism among employees, especially where rewards, recognition and promotions are concerned.

Effective leaders make certain their actions, judgments and decisions are consistent and not based upon specific circumstances. Only when leaders demonstrate consistency over time can they build trust with employees, who then know they will always be treated fairly.

Respect

Trust is built upon a foundation of mutual respect for one another. If respect is absent, trust can never be achieved. Leaders can develop and foster respect by:

- Demonstrating a personal regard for individual employees' experience, expertise, knowledge, insight and perspectives concerning their jobs.
- Actively seeking feedback and employees' insight, perspective and opinions regarding important decisions.
- Actively involving employees in the decision making process.

- Demonstrating appreciation for employees' personal contributions to the success of the organization.
- Providing the training, resources and support employees need to competently perform their jobs.
- Demonstrating care and concern for employees' lives outside of the workplace.

Pride

Trust is fostered and nurtured by a sense of mutual pride in the work, quality and accomplishments of the organization. This builds organizational cohesiveness that bonds all employees together and strengthens trust in all involved. As workplace cohesiveness increases, so does a sense of trust in the organization and its people. Everyone feels they are working together, and each can be trusted to fulfill his or her role and responsibilities.

Leaders can encourage the development of pride by using the following strategies:

- Helping employees understand their individual role in the organization and how their efforts contribute to its success.
- Helping them understand that they personally make a difference within the organization.
- Exhorting employees to take satisfaction both in their organization's accomplishments and its contributions to their community.

Comradery

Comradery is not normally associated with the concept of trust, yet it does contribute to the organizational cohesiveness established by trust. As cited above, the stronger the organizational cohesiveness, the stronger the bond between leaders and employees. All involved feel linked by common goals, experiences and successes. They have a sense that everyone is "in it together" and work as a unit rather than as individuals.

Leaders can use the following strategies to build comradery with their employees:

- Creating a workplace where a common concern is demonstrated and employees feel they can "be themselves."
- Openly and regularly celebrating special events and mutual successes.
- Consistently and openly recognizing, rewarding and celebrating individual successes in a warm and genuine manner.

POINTS TO PONDER — SOMETHING TO THINK ABOUT

1. Have you considered the five components discussed to be part of an atmosphere of trust?
2. Can you see how trust is undermined if one of the components is missing?

TRAINING ACTIVITY — APPLICATION & ACTION PLAN

1. Evaluate the atmosphere of trust within your organization. Take a sheet of paper and list the following components:
   - Credibility
   - Fairness
   - Respect
   - Pride
   - Comradery
2. Objectively evaluate the prevalence of each component in turn. Identify gaps and determine the specific strategies needed to address them.

6

When Trust Is Broken

There are many companies and organizations where the concept of trust is either considered unimportant and overlooked out of ignorance or has been damaged or destroyed by acts of betrayal by both leaders and employees. The ramifications of a missing or destroyed sense of trust can be far-reaching in terms of wasted human capital and negative impact on the company's bottom line.

An atmosphere where trust is damaged or absent is characterized by a lack of confidence, respect, pride and organizational cohesiveness. The consequences of these missing components are conflict, unrest, instability and an overall lack of effectiveness, efficiency and productivity.

Undoubtedly there are managers who thrive in this atmosphere. Most employ a "divide and conquer" management philosophy in order to gain an illusion of personal control and power. This approach thrives on employees' misery and unhappiness to satisfy personal agendas, and is wholly incompatible with an empowered organization.

IMPLICATIONS – WHAT THIS MEANS TO YOU

This is important for leaders, because without creating trust they cannot guide and direct their organization to greater heights of effectiveness and productivity. Empowered leaders are the antithesis of the divide and conquer manager who is only interested in the power and control they can garner irrespective of the price paid by their employees and their company.

STRATEGIES, TIPS & TECHNIQUES TO APPLY

When leaders fail to create and foster an atmosphere of trust or allow it to be damaged or destroyed, they are surrendering their leadership role, as its basis has been effectively removed. Instead they have taken the mantle of a manager of an organization plagued by:

Increased Conflict

Lack of credibility, respect and fairness is a breeding ground for every conceivable form of conflict. In the absence of trust, an "us vs. them" atmosphere prevails where employees don't believe the words and actions of management. This results in varying levels of labor unrest.

Additionally, lack of trust creates personal conflicts and problems both between managers and subordinates and among employees. It forces leaders to waste time settling petty disputes and babysitting employee problems. This saps their ability to focus on the more important issues impacting productivity and profitability.

Lack of Communication

Diminished or nonexistent trust affects overall communication in the organization. Since management doesn't trust employees, they are reluctant to share important information with them. Additionally, employees are resistant to sharing their own information, insights and perspectives that can help management make more qualified decisions ultimately leading to a better product or service. As problems persist, communication continues to suffer.

Increased Gossip

The vacuum created by a lack of communication is filled by harmful, toxic rumors. Individual reputations are damaged and overall performance is diminished by the effects of gossip among employees. Since employees feel they cannot trust either the company or its managers, their trust is placed in rumor and innuendo. This can completely undermine the effectiveness and cohesion of an organization.

Increased Personal Problems

When the working environment is destabilized by an atmosphere void of trust, companies experience an increase in absenteeism, employee turnover, theft, sabotage, lawsuits and a host of other problems that bleed the company's time, effectiveness, profitability and resources. As these problems continue and fester, mistrust is compounded—and plunges the company into deeper and more looming difficulties.

This atmosphere often leads quality employees to leave for a more stable working environment, leaving behind problematic employees who only cause further difficulties for the company.

Increased Quality Problems

As problems continue, employee attitudes and morale are affected, resulting in a decrease in overall product quality. This ultimately impacts the customer and can result in a marked loss of business.

Since the atmosphere of mistrust fosters poor morale and personal attitudes, employees lose their sense of pride, organizational cohesiveness and comradery. Concern over the loss of business and profitability is replaced by self-serving preservation of personal power and job security.

The overall result can be a death spiral for a company unless leadership can rebuild trust and restore its former status as a quality provider of products or services.

Reduced Productivity

The ultimate result of a lack of trust is an overall loss of productivity. In some instances, problems have become so overwhelming for a company that facilities have been closed, jobs lost and operations shifted to other locations.

The impact of a loss of trust and its ramifications cannot be overemphasized because of the dramatic and often overwhelming effect it can have on the organization. It won't only undermine the ability to lead, but ultimately can cause to an organization's downfall.

POINTS TO PONDER — SOMETHING TO THINK ABOUT

1. What have been your experiences when trust was missing or destroyed by betrayal?
2. Have you ever betrayed your employees' trust? What were the consequences?

TRAINING ACTIVITY — APPLICATION & ACTION PLAN

1. Evaluate your own organization to determine if you can identify problems or potential problems in each of the following areas:
    - Increased conflict
    - Lack of communication
    - Increased gossip
    - Increased personal problems
    - Increased quality problems
    - Reduced productivity
2. Identify specific actions that must be taken to eliminate these problems before they turn into major crises within your company.

7

Using an Ethics Decision Making Tool

Trust-building has more far-reaching implications than any other factor in the workplace. This is especially true where decision making is concerned. Leaders are making decisions that impact both employees and customers alike and that define the organization in their eyes. Leadership depends upon a leader's ability to generate trust and credibility in his or her words and actions.

IMPLICATIONS — WHAT THIS MEANS TO YOU

Trust and credibility are the basis of leadership. These elements are defined by the decisions a leader makes. Leaders are fully aware of the impact their decisions have upon their ability to effectively lead their organization. Inconsistent, faulty or poor decision making skills will undermine the trust and credibility leaders have developed.

If employees cannot trust the words and actions of a leader, the leader has lost his or her ability to lead. There is no basis for leadership. At this point, the basis for effective management is also destroyed. As individuals in this position can only manage by fear and intimidation, they will produce minimal results.

STRATEGIES, TIPS & TECHNIQUES TO APPLY

Decision making is a complex process, even when decisions appear simple. Leaders automatically go through a process that takes into consideration a series of factors involved in the development of a fair and balanced decision.

Truth

Before they make any determination, leaders must make sure they are dealing with the facts surrounding a situation or an event—not subjective opinions and perceptions. This includes ensuring all parties affected by a specific decision agree not only upon the pertinent facts but the veracity of the way in which the situation has been portrayed.

Arriving at an agreement on the truth of an issue is not as simple as it may seem. Personal agendas and internal politics can often alter one's view of the truth and taint the entire process. Leaders must become adept at objective fact-finding and develop the personal skills to separate reality from opinion.

Without this critical element, all decisions will be undermined by being based upon supposition rather than fact, and therefore, faulty.

Credible

Leaders must examine not only the truth of the available facts but also the credibility of the information and its sources. It is not uncommon for information presented as truth to be based upon rumor and supposition. While the information is perceived as truthful, it is not considered credible due to unreliable sources. Consequently leaders must consider not only the reliability of the information presented to them but also the credibility of the source.

Fair

Leaders must ensure that any decisions they make are equitable to all involved. This means that no favoritism is shown toward one party over another and that the consequence of a decision, whether positive or negative, impacts all individuals equally.

When decisions are made that do in fact impact one party more than another, leaders must assure that the criteria used for making their decision treats all parties fairly without bias or impartiality.

Respect

Leaders must assure that when making decisions, all interested parties are given equal opportunity and access to make their case. Leaders should respect their feedback, insight, opinion and perspective. Leaders should give them equal consideration during the decision making process.

Comradery

An additional ramification of a leader's decision making is the impact on comradery within the organization. When leaders make decisions fairly and without bias, they should enhance comradery in the organization. This occurs because the credibility of the decision is enhanced and it is considered fair, truthful, and to promote good will throughout the organization.

Beneficial

The final aspect of the principles of trust in decision making is the need for leaders to make certain that their decisions are beneficial to all individuals concerned without bias or favoritism.

Rotary International promotes an easy to remember decision making tool. The use of this tool builds trust and ethical decision making and incorporates all of the elements discussed in this lesson.

The FOUR-WAY TEST of the things we think, say or do:

1. Is it the TRUTH?
2. Is it FAIR to all concerned?
3. Will it build GOODWILL and BETTER FRIENDSHIPS?
4. Will it be BENEFICIAL to all concerned?

POINTS TO PONDER — SOMETHING TO THINK ABOUT

1. Do you as a habit consider all of the elements of truth in your decision making?
2. What additional elements do you include in your decision making?

TRAINING ACTIVITY — APPLICATION & ACTION PLAN

Apply the Four-Way Test to all of your decisions for the next thirty days and determine if it has an impact.

1. Is it the TRUTH?
2. Is it FAIR to all concerned?
3. Will it build GOODWILL and BETTER FRIENDSHIPS?
4. Will it be BENEFICIAL to all concerned?

8

Cohesiveness: The Key to Effective Leadership

The concept of organizational cohesiveness is recognized in the military as a factor that makes or breaks unit effectiveness. Military leaders have long recognized that when cohesiveness breaks down and is left unaddressed, the unit's ability to perform is not simply diminished but ultimately destroyed. The same concept applies within organizations.

Organizational cohesiveness is achieved when all members of the organization have reached the point where they are working closely together as a single unit toward the accomplishment of mutual goals and objectives without regard to personal agendas and attitudes.

IMPLICATIONS — WHAT THIS MEANS TO YOU

By establishing trust leaders take a diverse collection of individuals and blend them into an efficient working unit. When this occurs, and leaders have built and are nurturing organizational cohesiveness, they will have accomplished their primary goals. This is a most satisfying and beneficial position for leaders to be in.

STRATEGIES, TIPS & TECHNIQUES TO APPLY

Leaders build and foster trust not only among their employees and themselves, but between all members of the organizational unit. Cohesiveness is established and is reinforced over time because bonds of trust among individual members of the organization are strengthened. Each individual learns how he or she is able to trust the other members in the attainment of individual and organizational goals.

When leaders are able to establish strong organizational cohesiveness, the following elements are found:

Teamwork

When organizational cohesiveness is achieved, leaders see an overall increase in team development. Individual employees are able to work in self-directed groups to tackle specific problems, concerns and issues that need to be resolved if the organization is to progress and meet its objectives.

In many organizations, this is a major shift in thinking and personal attitudes. Employees and leaders think in terms of the team and organization, replacing their own personal goals and agendas with those of the organization.

Individual Contribution

It has been recognized that any individual within any company or organization can contribute ideas and insights as to how to improve quality, performance and productivity in the position they hold. Yet these individuals are generally reluctant to volunteer this information, primarily because they have not been asked in the past, and have therefore concluded their contributions are unwanted.

When organizational cohesiveness is achieved, many of these barriers are removed and leaders will see an overall increase in individual employee contributions. Since they are motivated by the success of the team or organization, they feel more open to contribute feedback, observations, insights, perspectives and ideas to assist them. When this occurs, and more individuals are motivated to personally contribute, a synergy is achieved that amplifies the power of these ideas, increases brainstorming, and infuses the organization with new and creative thinking.

Empowerment

A workplace environment that is built on trust and thus fosters organizational cohesiveness also builds empowered employees. The sense of trust between leaders and employees empowers them to make more independent decisions and work more freely in groups and teams since they are working toward common organizational goals and objectives. The concepts of trust and empowerment are codependent, feeding and building upon each other, strengthening over time.

Cooperation

While teamwork, empowerment and organizational cohesion all require collaboration between leaders and employees as well as among employees, within a cohesive organizational unit, there are levels of cooperation among individuals, departments, vendors and customers that cannot be minimized. These levels of cooperation are beyond the scope of individual responsibilities, yet are clearly visible and significantly contribute to the success of the organization. They are reflective of "team spirit," organizational pride and employee comradery. It is noticed by outsiders, helps define the organization and is the first thing to suffer when organizational cohesiveness is disrupted or destroyed.

Leaders should note this sense of cooperation when they have achieved effective levels of organizational cohesiveness and actively monitor it as an overall indicator of unit, division or company health.

Quality

Another easily discernable benefit of organizational cohesiveness is the increase in the quality of unit work and individual contributions. The organization has been able to maximize its efficiency, as an increase in overall product or service quality often translates into fewer defective and rejected units. This reduces the time required to rework faulty units and increases the organization's efficiency and profitability.

POINTS TO PONDER — SOMETHING TO THINK ABOUT

1. Are you committed to the development of a cohesive organizational unit?
2. Can you see the benefits of working within a cohesive organizational unit?

TRAINING ACTIVITY — APPLICATION & ACTION PLAN

Examine your organizational unit and identify the specific barriers preventing you from building and nurturing organizational cohesion.

1. Consider the areas of trust, credibility, teamwork, empowerment, individual contributions and cooperation, and isolate difficulties that are preventing you or the organization from achieving cohesiveness.
2. Determine how you can remove or minimize the obstacles you have discovered.
3. Create an action plan to move your organization forward and increase overall cohesiveness.

About the Author

Timothy F. Bednarz, Ph.D. is CEO of the American Management Development Group, Inc. For over 20 years he has researched, designed and authored hundreds of learning and development programs used by Fortune 1000 companies.

He is also the author of *Great! What Makes Leaders Great. What They Did, How They Did It and What You Can Learn from It* (2011).

Speaking Availability

Timothy F. Bednarz, Ph.D. is available for speaking engagements for your next meeting or association event. He can be contacted at 800-654-4935 or by e-mail at timothy.bednarz@majorium.com.

Bulk Sales

Bulk sales of this book or any other titles available from Majorium Business Press. Inquiries can be directed to sales@majorium.com, or by phone at 800-6654-4935.

Quick Order Form

Fax orders: 715-342-1118. Send this form.

Telephone orders: Call 800-654-4935 toll-free. Have your credit card ready.

Email orders: sales@majorium.com

Postal orders: Majorium Business Press, 2025 Main Street, Stevens Point, WI 54481, USA.

Please send the following books:

____

____

____

____

Please send more FREE information on:

❑Catalog ❑Speaking/Seminars ❑Mailing Lists ❑Consulting

Name: ____

Address: ____

City: ____________________________ State: _____ Zip: __________

Telephone: ____

Email address: ____

Sales tax: Please add 5.5% for products shipped to Wisconsin addresses.

Shipping by air:

United States: $4.00 for first book and $2.00 for each additional product.

International: $9.00 for first book; $5.00 for each additional product (estimate).

Made in United States
Cleveland, OH
06 November 2026

47678358R10030